ALZHEIMER'S DISEASE

ALZHEIMER'S
DISEASE

Marlene Targ Brill

BENCHMARK BOOKS

MARSHALL CAVENDISH
NEW YORK

Benchmark Books
Marshall Cavendish
99 White Plains Road
Tarrytown, New York 10591-9001
www.marshallcavendish.com

Library of Congress Cataloging-in-Publication Data
Brill, Marlene Targ.
  Alzheimer's disease / Marlene Targ Brill.
      p. cm. — (Health alert)
  Includes bibliographical references and index.
  ISBN 0-7614-1799-0
  1. Alzheimer's disease—Juvenile literature. I. Title. II. Series: Health alert (Benchmark Books)

  RC523.3.B75 2005
  616.8'31—dc22

                          2004006528

Front cover: A colored MRI of the brain of an Alzheimer's patient
Title page: Nerve cells

Photo research by Regina Flanagan

Front cover: Simon Fraser / Photo Researchers, Inc.

The photographs in this book are used by permission and through the courtesy of:
Photo Researchers, Inc.: David Gifford, 11; John Bavosi, 12; Science Photo Library, 13, 26; Veronique Estiot, 14; Simon Fraser, 15, 41; A. Pasieka, 17; Tissuepix, 19; Dr. Robert Friedland, 20; Deep Light Productions, 25; Zephyr, 27; Mehau Kulyk, 28; BSIP Mendil, 29, 31, 51; National Institute of Health, 34; Will & Deni McIntyre, 40, 43, 50; CC Studio, 45; Rosenfeld Images Ltd, 47. *Corbis:* 38, 55; Bettmann, 39; John Henley, 22; Michael Maslan Historic Photographs, 37; Randy Faris, 46. *Custom Medical Stock Photo:* 53.

Printed in China

6 5 4 3 2 1

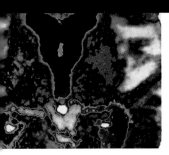

CONTENTS

1

WHAT IS IT LIKE TO HAVE ALZHEIMER'S DISEASE?

Adam thought his grandmother was awesome. She rarely missed his sports games or his school performances. After school, she often helped him with homework, or baked delicious cookies. She never complained that his room looked messy or that his pants were too big and baggy. His grandmother was very patient with him and she never yelled at him when he forgot to mow the lawn.

Sometimes Adam and his grandmother went camping or boating. They laughed a lot and made jokes that only they shared. His grandmother often helped him solve problems and made him feel better when he was feeling blue. Sometimes Adam felt closer to his grandmother than to his parents.

Then Adam's grandmother started to change. She would sometimes forget a few things, such as where she parked the car at the grocery store. She would also forget things she had promised. At first, Adam hardly noticed. He knew everyone was forgetful now and then. And his grandmother was older, and it was normal for people to forget things as they aged.

But soon Adam noticed differences he could not explain. Normally, his grandmother dressed neatly. Now she appeared scruffy. Her clothes were messy and very wrinkled. Her hair looked like she had not brushed or washed it in weeks. Her behavior changed also. She could no longer remember some of their jokes. And she seemed confused or upset when Adam asked for homework help. One day Grandma forgot to take cookies out of the oven, and they burned. Her mind drifted to earlier times, sometimes to many years before Adam was even born. Adam finally had to admit something was wrong when his grandmother did not recognize him.

Adam talked to his best friend Jose. Jose understood how Adam felt. When Jose's grandfather lived with Jose's family, he would also forget a lot of things. Jose's grandfather often wore two different shoes or put his pants on backward. As time passed, his grandfather stopped shaving. He stopped using spoons and forks and started eating with his fingers. A few times, Jose's grandfather snuck out of the house. He would wander around the neighborhood calling for Jose's grandmother, who had died four years earlier. Once, the police found him roaming the streets three miles away. Another time, he knocked on a neighbor's door down the street and asked, "Where am I?" Even though he had lived in the neighborhood for thirty years, Jose's grandfather often had no idea where he was or how he got there.

Adam wondered what had happened to their grandparents. "My grandfather had Alzheimer's Disease. It is a disease that destroys parts of the brain," Jose told Adam. "Your grandmother might have it, too."

Adam shared his worries with his family. They took his grandmother to the doctor. The doctor ran many tests and examined her to see how she was doing. The doctors said that she had Alzheimer's Disease. Alzheimer's Disease is a brain disease that affects a person's mind. Because of physical and chemical changes in the brain, people with the disease act differently. Eventually, too many changes occur in a person's brain and he or she dies. Unfortunately, there is no cure. But scientists and doctors have tried giving patients different treatments to slow the disease and to make the patient more comfortable.

Adam's grandmother was given special medication, but there was nothing that Adam or his family could do to stop the disease. The best thing they could do was offer help and support.

They watched her more carefully, helped her take her medicine, and took her to doctors' appointments. When she became too sick to wash or dress herself, they helped her with that too. They still spent time talking with her, no matter what she talked about—even when it made no sense. When she was no longer able to speak clearly or to recognize them, they still continued to let her know how much they cared about her. She was still an important part of their family, and they loved her.

2

WHAT IS ALZHEIMER'S DISEASE?

Alzheimer's disease is a cruel disease that steals lives. It's hard to know what to expect. The years of exchanging memories of old age are gone. It's a long, long good-bye.

—Nancy Reagan, former First Lady

Alzheimer's Disease (which is often referred to as AD) is sometimes known as the forgetting disease. The most obvious **symptom** (sign) of AD is a person's loss of memory and his or her inability to understand where or who he or she is. This is more serious than forgetting a few names or losing your keys. Once symptoms appear, they worsen over time. Eventually those with AD die as the brain suffers more damage.

THE BRAIN

Alzheimer's Disease affects the brain. The brain is the main control center in the human body. It controls such things as feelings, senses (smell, touch, taste, hearing), speech, memory, breathing, and movement. When AD attacks the brain, a person can lose the ability to function. To understand the disease, it is important to know what the human brain is like and how it functions.

An adult brain can weigh less than 3 pounds.

The brain has many grooves and is sort of soft and spongy. It is protected by the hard bones of the skull. Though the brain only accounts for a very small part of the body, it requires nearly 20 percent of the body's blood and oxygen. The brain uses these **nutrients** to carry out the important functions that keep a person alive.

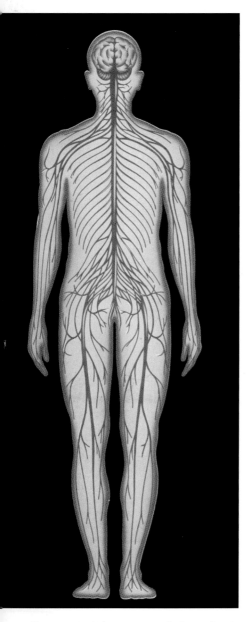

Nerves stretch across and throughout the body.

The brain has many different parts and can be divided into different regions. Each area of the brain performs a different job. For example, one part allows people to see, while another controls moving or feeling.

The brain is made of billions of tiny nerve cells. Nerve cells are also called neurons. Neurons contain substances called proteins. These proteins help cells do their job. They are especially important for cell growth and repair. (Different proteins are found throughout the body—not just in the brain.) The job of the neurons is to carry messages back and forth between the brain and other parts of the body. They do this through a complex network of nerve fibers commonly referred to as nerves.

Nerves stretch throughout all parts of the body. Signals are sent back and forth through this nerve network. For example, if you closed your eyes, reached into a bag with dimes and quarters, and grabbed a dime, you could probably tell that it is a dime without looking at it. This is because nerves in your hand send messages to your brain that describe the coin. These messages have information about how large the coin is, how thick it is, or how heavy it feels. Your brain receives these messages and comes to the conclusion that it is, in fact, a dime. In healthy people, this message relay occurs very quickly.

Your brain is constantly receiving and responding to signals throughout your body. Even while you are sleeping, your brain is working hard. The brain is also responsible for actions you do not think about. These include breathing, making the heart pump, and digesting food.

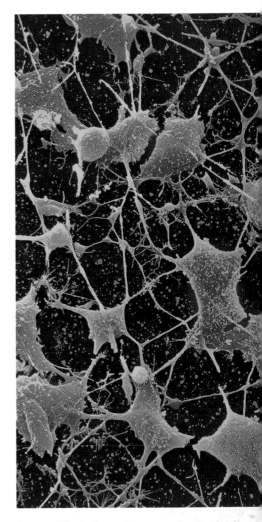

A magnified view of neurons in the brain.

Neurons share information with each other and with the rest of the body. They do this by producing and giving off certain chemicals called **neurotransmitters**. There are very small gaps between nerves. Neurotransmitters travel from the end of one

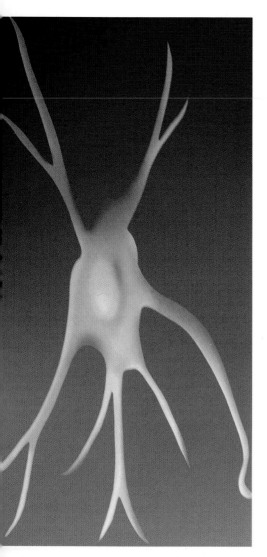

A neuron has many different parts. The structures that branch out of the neuron's central cell body are the dendrites and one axon. The dendrites conduct messages to the neuron. The axon sends the messages out of the neuron toward other neurons.

neuron across the gap to the end of another neuron. This is how messages are relayed.

When one neuron transmits information to another neuron, an information pathway is formed. These pathways act much like railroad tracks carrying trains, only these pathways carry signals. Once pathways are formed, signals can travel more easily throughout the nerve network. The brain constantly builds new pathways as neurotransmitters send millions of signals back and forth. Learning stimulates new pathways. The more new information people learn, the more tracks grow between neurons in their brains. This information is not only knowledge they might learn in school or from a book. Pathways are formed when a person learns a new skill or moves or reacts in new ways.

WHAT GOES WRONG

The exact cause of Alzheimer's Disease is unknown. The one thing that doctors do know is that AD is not contagious. You cannot catch the disease like you would catch the flu or a cold.

Research has shown that nerve cells of people with AD do not function properly. They cannot carry messages or send signals. One reason for this failure is a buildup of extra protein in brain tissue. In a healthy brain, unused protein is absorbed back into the body, and the protein levels are normal and safe. In AD, nerve cells produce too much protein that does not get absorbed. The sticky clumps of unused protein form **plaques**. These plaques get in the way of healthy nerve cells and message relays.

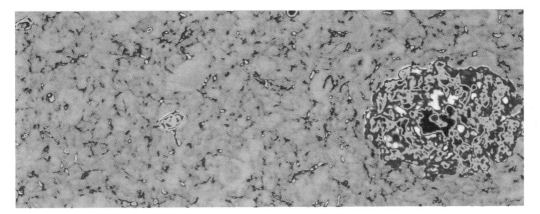

A brain tissue sample from an Alzheimer's patient. The small purple structures are healthy nerve cells. The pink and blue clumps are the plaques and tangles that interfere with normal brain function.

Another problem in AD involves bunches of damaged nerve endings. These produce threadlike tangles in the brain. The tangles prevent messages from traveling between nerve cells. Neurotransmitters are unable to carry messages to other brain cells. They act like derailed trains that cannot travel across the tracks from place to place. Without proper connections, neurons stop working. When many neurons stop working, the brain begins to lose the ability to perform specific functions.

Damaged brain cells shrink and slowly die. As damage spreads, brain size decreases. In AD, the part of the brain that controls memory stops working first. This is why loss of memory is often the first sign of Alzheimer's Disease. An important chemical for memory is the neurotransmitter acetylcholine. As the disease progresses, production of acetylcholine decreases. Scientists do not know if low levels of acetylcholine cause the disease or are the result of it.

Regions of the brain that are involved in self-control and emotions are the next to fail. Some areas of the brain, such as the part that is responsible for eyesight, never die. No one knows why AD affects some parts of the brain and not others. Many believe that it might have to do with the role of certain proteins.

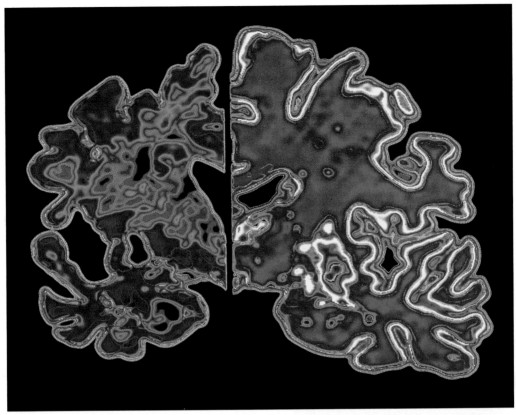

This computer image shows samples of tissue from a healthy brain (right) and a brain affected by Alzheimer's Disease (left). The AD brain tissue is smaller because the disease has killed many nerve cells. As brain tissue dies, normal brain functions worsen.

Family History

Some cases of AD may be related to whether or not people in a person's family had the disease. Studies reveal that AD in people younger than age 65 runs in families. The greater risk among relatives comes from **genes** that are passed from parent to child. Genes are the tiniest bit of information that

Who Gets AD?

....

Signs of Alzheimer's Disease appear in men and women of all races throughout the world. For some reason, however, AD strikes twice as many women as men. Some studies have shown that African Americans and Hispanics are also more likely than Caucasians—whites—to develop the disease.

But with all people, the risk of developing AD doubles every five years after age 60. The greatest threat of AD is to people over age 85. The National Institute on Aging is the government agency concerned with issues that affect older adults. Institute reports claim that AD affects about one in ten adults between ages 75 and 85 and almost one in two people over age 85. However, a small number of people— about 20,000—experience AD in their thirties or forties. These cases usually stem from a strong family history of the disease striking younger people.

determine human features, such as eye color or diseases like AD. Each human cell has between 50,000 and 100,000 genes. Together they contain all details needed for a person to develop before and after being born.

A problem in one or more genes can change a person's life. With AD, researchers find that certain genes alter how cells make proteins. This, in turn, might affect the production of tangles and plaques in the brain. So far, three genes have been linked to a greater threat of early AD. Children who have one parent with either of these genes have a 50 percent greater chance of getting the disease. Still, early development of the disease only accounts for about 5 percent of AD cases.

One other gene has been linked to the risk of AD after age 65. Even with this gene, the threat of getting AD from relatives depends upon how much younger than 85 they are when the disease occurred.

Head Injury

Studies show that the chance of developing AD increases in people who suffer head injuries serious enough to knock them out. In 2000, scientists checked medical records of 548 former soldiers who had head injuries. They found that those who had passed out due to head injury were twice as

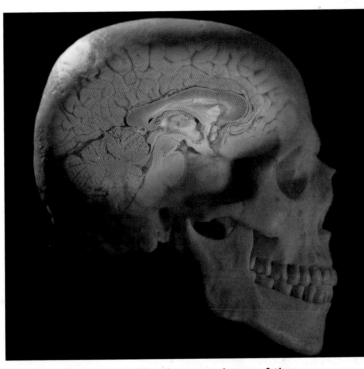

Despite being protected by the strong bones of the skull, a brain can still become bruised and damaged.

likely to show signs of AD later. The risk of AD rose with more serious injury and longer blackouts. Not everyone who has been knocked unconscious will develop AD, but researchers continue to investigate this theory.

Lifestyle

Many other factors contribute to longer-lasting brain health. When investigating AD, doctors look at overall health, diet, exercise, and pollution in the environment.

Education. An old saying goes, "If you don't use it you lose it." This may apply to brain health and Alzheimer's Disease. Several studies suggest that people who are less mentally active and have the least amount of formal education (attending school) increase their risk of developing AD. One study tracked adults who had less than seven years of formal

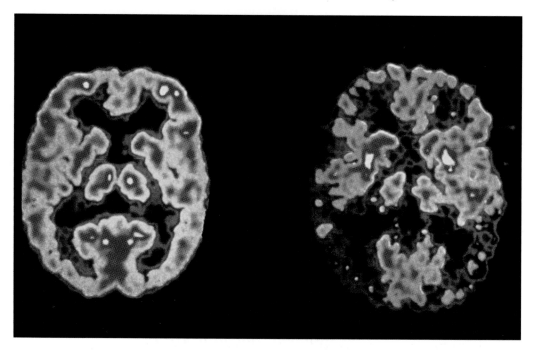

This scan shows a healthy brain (left) and the brain of an Alzheimer's patient (right). The red and yellow indicate high brain activity. An Alzheimer's brain is considerably less active than a normal, healthy brain.

education. The results show that these people were more than six times more likely to develop AD than people who had more than seven years of formal education. From this, scientists draw the conclusion that exercising your brain by learning new things is one way to keep it healthy. It is important to keep in mind, however, that formal education is not the only way to stimulate your brain. Activities such as reading and doing puzzles can also help to keep your brain healthy and active.

Diet and Exercise. Studies also point to improper diet and being overweight as risk factors. Many claim that eating a high-fat diet contributes to greater risk of AD. Diets without certain vitamins result in almost the same risk. For example, low levels of the vitamins **folate** and B12 in the blood contribute to twice as much memory loss and confusion.

Regular exercise can help to keep the body healthy. Exercising strengthens muscles and bones while also helping a person maintain a healthy weight. Studies have shown that exercising stimulates the brain to release special chemicals. These chemicals can help the body stay healthy. They can also make a person feel better and happier.

However, it is important for everybody to check with their doctor to make sure that they are doing the right amount and

Exercise is good for people of all ages.

the right type of exercise. Too much exercise can cause harm—especially to someone who is already suffering from an illness.

Illness. Some AD studies involve looking at the brain tissue of women who had brain damage that occurred as a result of illness. Their brains had formed scars from the damage. These scars indicate that blood flow to the brain had been interrupted. This caused decreased or **abnormal** brain function. These same women who had scarred brains also showed signs of AD. Researchers believe that there is a strong connection. Now questions arise about whether brain injury from other illnesses can cause AD or merely makes it worse in someone who was going to develop the disease anyway.

Doctors are beginning to compare AD with several brain diseases or ongoing infections and illnesses. Heart disease is considered another possible risk factor for AD, as are some slow-acting **viruses.** Studies that link proteins or damaged genes to diseases help scientists learn more about how AD advances.

Environmental Factors. Scientists know the environment can affect AD, but they are unsure how. One study followed identical twin girls who shared the same genes and received the same upbringing. As adults one developed AD, while the other did not.

Since the women had the same family situation, questions of what caused the disease focused on risk factors in the environment. Did the twin with AD have infections that the other did not? Was she exposed to more aluminum or other chemicals and minerals that are currently being investigated as possible causes of AD? Did she eat too many foods containing sugar substitutes, high fats, or other products harmful to the body? Scientists hope that continued research will help to answer some of these questions.

DIAGNOSING ALZHEIMER'S DISEASE

As with all illnesses, it is important to visit a doctor who can figure out what is wrong. Those who are diagnosed with early AD can take advantage of new treatments and medications that may slow the disease. They can use the extra time they have to live fuller lives. They can adjust their goals and

Dementia

Several medical conditions besides AD can cause dementia. Many of these conditions can be treated if discovered early. These conditions may include

- Vision or hearing problems
- Alcohol abuse
- Depression
- Cancer in the brain (brain tumors)
- Heart, lung, or circulation (blood) problems
- Head injury
- A reaction to medication
- Chemical imbalances in the body

have a say in planning for their future.

But early AD is tough to identify. Doctors must sort through the signs of forgetting that happen to healthy people, too. There are other illnesses that may cause the **dementia** (a weakening of thinking skills that interferes with daily living) that AD causes. It is important to visit a doctor because many non-Alzheimer's causes of dementia are treatable.

Unfortunately, the only way to definitively identify AD is to examine a person's brain tissue after he or she has died. Still, doctors and other specialists can come close to identifying AD by asking questions and conducting physical exams.

Asking Questions

To test someone's forgetfulness, doctors ask questions about past and current physical and mental health. They want to know about medicines the patient takes. They may need to know if some of the patient's medication is causing the dementia. Doctors will ask about family medical history and if other relatives have suffered from AD or dementia. Doctors often talk with family members or close friends to confirm the patient's answers because people with AD may not realize how much they are forgetting.

Physical Exams

A complete exam looks for different health problems that may seem like AD. The doctor takes blood pressure readings, measures a person's pulse, and asks about diet. Blood and urine tests are also used to explore vitamin or chemical imbalances.

The patient may go to a hospital or clinic for special scans. Different scans look into the brain and check how it is working. An electroencephalogram (EEG) tracks brain activity. Wires from the EEG machine are taped to a person's head. These wires can sense brain activity. The wires send the brain activity to the

A neurologist—a doctor who specializes in the nervous system—monitors a patient's brain waves using an EEG machine.

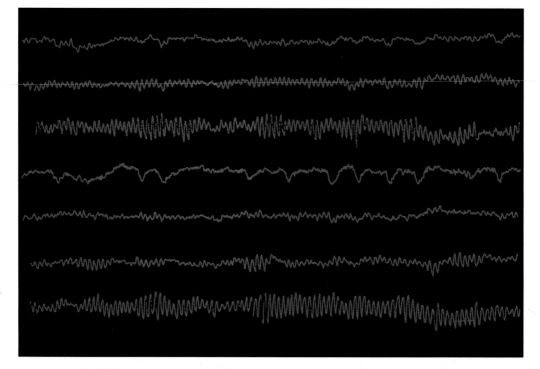

A healthy EEG brain wave pattern. The brain waves of an Alzheimer's patient would be flatter, with fewer dips and spikes.

machine. The machine prints out waves that show a pattern. This pattern of brain waves indicates whether or not nerves in the brains are sending and receiving messages. Doctors and technicians are trained to read the waves and determine what the problem may be.

A CAT scan (computerized axial tomography) is a scan that is more detailed than an X ray. CAT scans are also called CT scans. The scans can be performed on different parts of the body. Before a CAT scan of the brain is done, a patient receives a shot of dye. The patient then goes through the CAT scan machine. The machine produces a picture of the brain. The dye highlights specific portions of the brain during the CAT scan. These parts are visible when the scan is finished. The CAT scan can show brain damage from blood clots, illness, cancer or other medical problems.

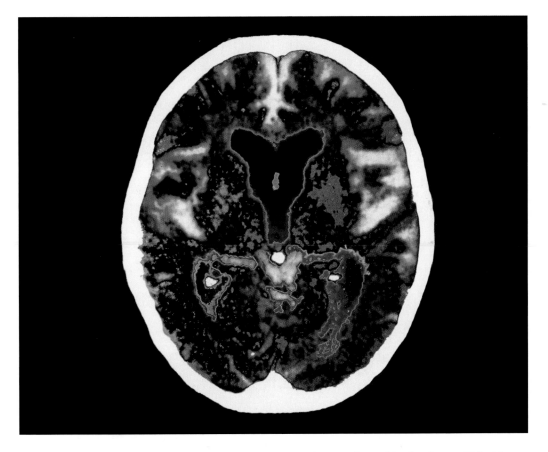

The pink areas in this colored CAT scan display the destruction of brain tissue. This AD patient has little healthy brain tissue (green) left.

Newer scans have provided breakthroughs in detecting AD. The scans look into the brain to highlight detailed pictures of the individual structures. An MRI (magnetic resonance imaging) displays cross-sections of the brain that show

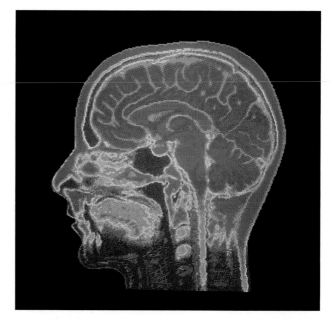

This MRI shows a section of a healthy brain. MRIs are painless scans that can help doctors determine what is wrong inside the body.

details of the different parts. PET (positron emission tomography) and SPECT (single photon emission computed tomography) reveal activity within the brain. Researchers hope to use these types of scans to **diagnose** AD before it gets to the later stages.

Another hospital test that doctors might use to diagnose AD is a spinal tap. Fluid is drawn from the **spine** by a long needle. The fluid is then tested for infection or illness. The fluid may also show high levels of proteins linked to AD. However, major problems with this test are the pain involved and possible side effects from the procedure.

Doctors are exploring the idea of smell as a painless test for AD. In one study, nineteen of forty-seven people with memory problems had difficulty identifying different smells. Sixteen of the nineteen claimed they had a good sense of smell, although tests showed otherwise. Doctors believe that losing the sense of smell and not realizing the sense is gone may be one way to predict AD. But more research is needed using smell as a sign of AD.

Mental Exams

If exams and tests fail to find a medical problem, patients go through exercises to judge how well their brain works. They are given mental tests and activities that measure memory, reasoning, language skills, and the ability to perform math and movement tasks. Patients may be asked to name simple objects, repeat

Written tests might be a part of an examination to see if a patient has Alzheimer's Disease.

lists of words, remember clues from earlier in the session, copy designs, and draw simple shapes and pictures.

Warning Signs

....

The Alzheimer's Association has prepared a list of common warning signs for AD. Most of the items on the list cause everyone trouble at some time. But with AD, symptoms must be serious enough to alter work, daily activities, and social interactions.

- Memory problems that are not normal; one example is forgetting how to fix breakfast
- Difficulty speaking and writing; forgetting simple words or substituting other words that may not make sense
- Poor judgment, such as wearing slippers outdoors on snowy days
- Extreme cases of misplacing things: placing the checkbook in the freezer or grapes in the washing machine
- Mood swings
- Personality changes
- A loss of energy
- Trouble performing familiar tasks
- Problems with higher level thinking skills, such as reasoning and dealing with money and numbers
- Difficulty with place and time: not knowing were you are or the year you are living in

THE STAGES OF THE DISEASE

Each person's experience with AD is different, but scientists have determined that there are three main stages of the disease.

Early Stages

The first stages of AD are often difficult to spot. People find themselves forgetting more. They repeat activities because they do not remember that they had already completed the tasks. Alzheimer's patients may also get a nagging feeling that something is wrong, but they cannot identify what it might be. Many people just assume these symptoms are normal signs of aging. In some cases they are correct. But they may not realize that they are in the early stages of the disease.

AD begins with forgetting names, dates, and newly learned information. One person might forget how to get home from the store, another how to balance a checkbook. After each new memory loss, people with early AD become unusually nervous or restless from facing difficult situations. To limit the chance that they will forget things, they make lists to help them. Some avoid the demanding activities or settings altogether. "I can feel myself sliding down that slippery slope," AD patient Larry Rose wrote in his book *Show Me the Way to Go Home*. "I have a sadness and an anxiety that I have never experienced before. I keep pushing myself to use the abilities I have left."

As the disease progresses, an Alzheimer's patient might have problems identifying shapes and solving simple puzzles.

Middle Stages

As the disease progresses, people with AD experience more serious memory loss. They may remember events from long ago, but they cannot recall someone they just met recently or what they just did. They become confused more easily, and mix up times and places. A person with this stage of AD may forget how to do basic daily living skills, such as washing or dressing. Some people lose weight or become ill because they forget to eat or drink.

The worst forgetting involves how to get along with others. Most people with the disease experience a personality change. Some lose their sense of humor and can no longer make or understand jokes and funny comments. The kindest, most polite people may turn mean, throw tantrums, or become moody. They may cry one minute and start screaming the next. At first, these behaviors may reflect frustration and anger. Alzheimer's patients become upset when they can no longer do what once came naturally. Personality changes may also come from feelings of sadness and embarrassment.

As the disease advances, strange fears may surface. AD can trigger imaginary visions or dangers that healthy people do not see. Some AD patients may see, hear, smell, taste, or feel things that are unreal. Fears can be very scary and lead to pacing or staying awake at night.

Occasionally, people with AD seem to shut down—sitting and staring into space without emotion or interest in moving. They may shake, fall, or experience trouble walking, writing, and reading. These and other changes may come and go for a time. But they return as the disease progresses. In her book *Living in the Labyrinth*, AD patient Diana McGowin recalls, "Painfully lonely, I still sit . . . alone in my home. I am suspended. Somewhere there is that ever-present reminder list of what I am supposed to do today. But I cannot find it."

Late Stages

Alzheimer's Disease never goes away. The disease eventually erases the ability to learn, remember, think, and behave. People in late-stage AD are unable to recognize family members. They cannot stand, walk, or move about without help. Behavior turns more unpleasant and demanding. Some people who are going through the late stages of the disease are extremely quiet and do not interact with anybody.

Decreased brainpower results in a total loss of skills such as going to the bathroom at the appropriate time and place.

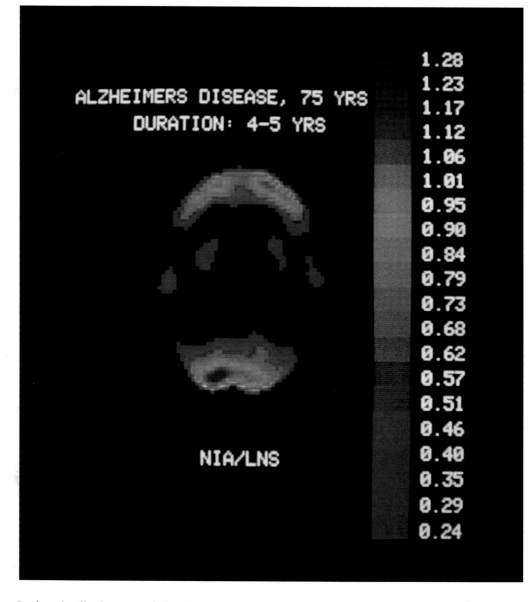

During the final stages of the disease, most of a patient's brain barely functions. In this scan the colored areas show brain activity, while the dark areas represent dead brain tissue.

Eventually a person might lose the ability to swallow or move at all. During the final stages of AD, patients stay in bed. But laying in bed for so long creates more problems. They cannot eat properly, their muscles become weak, or they may develop bedsores. These sores are injuries that come from lying in one position for too long.

As their brain function deteriorates, AD patients are more likely to become sick. Many patients die from ill nesses other than AD because their bodies were no longer able to fight infection. Others die as their organ systems fail. Unfortunately, the disease drags on until the totally helpless person dies. Alzheimer's is a painful disease that slowly robs a person of his or her life.

How Common is Alzheimer's Disease?

More than four million Americans live with the disease, and 377,000 new cases develop every year. In 2001 alone, 54,000 of those affected with AD died. This makes AD the fourth leading cause of death in America.

The number of deaths from AD is expected to triple by 2040. This is in part because the 76 million babies born between 1946 and 1956 (called Baby Boomers) are entering old age. People live longer nowadays, which further increases the risk of developing AD.

One hundred years ago, the average American lived 47 years. Today, average school-age kids can expect to live until age 77 or beyond. These figures translate into more cases of AD, and they mean more young people will encounter AD in their families.

3

THE HISTORY OF ALZHEIMER'S DISEASE

Scientists believe that age-related forgetting has been around since civilization began. Ancient writings talk about dementia. But for hundreds of years, however, people tended not to live beyond their fifties. Symptoms of brain disorder from aging and concern about the disorders were rare. Since there were fewer elderly people, no one really knew about diseases that mainly affected older people.

For centuries, no one knew what caused problems with thoughts and feelings. Most people did not realize that these problems were linked to brain illness or damage. It was commonly believed that people who behaved oddly or could not think properly were affected by evil spirits. Sometimes religious officials would be called in to chase the spirits away. But these "cures" did not work. Often, the troubled people would be shut away from society. They were locked in a room in a house, or in an insane asylum with many other mentally ill people. In most of these places, these people suffered through their illnesses without proper medical treatment.

For hundreds of years, scientists and doctors examined the inner organs of people who had died, hoping to see what had gone wrong. But without microscopes or other magnifying devices, the brain of a person with mental illness looked the same as a brain from someone who was healthy.

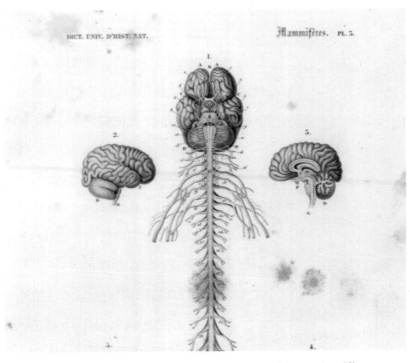

This sketch of the brain and spinal cord appeared in a scientific reference book from France in the late 1840s.

In 1907, a German physician named Alois Alzheimer made discoveries that explained some brain disorders. Alzheimer had examined a patient with memory problems. The patient also had increasing problems with her behavior. The woman did not understand many questions and she would sometimes stop speaking. She died after nearly five years of sickness. Alzheimer decided that the 51-year-old woman battled a form of dementia. When he examined her brain under a microscope, he discovered many brain cells gone. In their place were tangles and plaques. These two discoveries in someone so young signaled a new disease. This disease became known as Alzheimer's after the man who first reported it.

Throughout the 1900s, researchers identified a number of chemicals and cells that are somehow involved in Alzheimer's

Alzheimer worked in the laboratory of Emil Kraepelin, a leader in research on mental illness in the early 1900s.

Ronald Reagan is one of the most famous people to be stricken with AD. Knowledge of his illness helped to increase public awareness.

Famous People With Alzheimer's

••••••••••••••••••••••••••••••••••••

Alzheimer's Disease affects people from all walks of life. The condition attacks famous people as well as everyday folks. Some well-known people who lived with Alzheimer's include

- Rita Hayworth, actress
- Iris Murdoch, British author
- Aaron Copeland, American composer
- E. B. White, author of *Charlotte's Web*
- Sugar Ray Robinson, champion boxer

Disease. To increase public awareness of the need for continued research, the decade from 1990 to 2000 was named the "Decade of the Brain" by President George H.W. Bush and the United States Congress. More people found out about AD because many famous people are suffering from it. In 1994, former United States President Ronald Reagan revealed to the public that he was suffering from AD. Throughout his illness, his family helped to encourage the public to support Alzheimer's research. Reagan passed away in 2004.

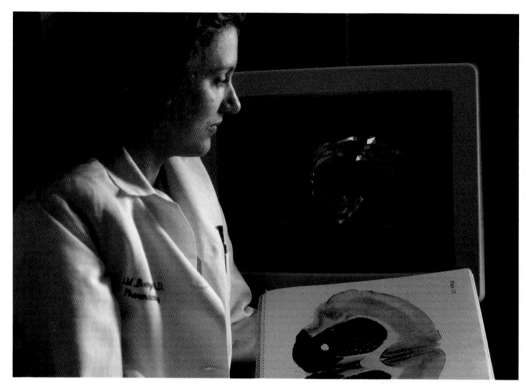

New theories and new technologies have allowed scientists to better understand Alzheimer's disease and other brain disorders.

New Discoveries

It recently was discovered that a small percentage of people inherit genes that make it more likely that they will get Alzheimer's Disease. But for most people, the exact cause is not known, and there is still no cure. Some other new ideas are being studied. These studies investigate how the immune system may be involved, or how vitamins and minerals may be helpful in preventing brain cell damage.

Advances in drug research have also helped. Drugs cannot prevent the disease, but they do reduce symptoms and sometimes keep the disease from getting worse. A **vaccine** is being developed but has not worked yet. Researchers have also found evidence that there may be cells in each person's brain that could replace those that have died due to AD. Until now, it was assumed that any brain cell that dies can never be replaced. Research continues and many hope to one day find ways to treat and prevent Alzheimer's Disease.

By examining brain cells and chemicals, scientists may someday find a way to prevent or cure Alzheimer's.

4

DEALING WITH ALZHEIMER'S DISEASE

Alzheimer's snatches some people's minds quickly while allowing others years of independence. With time, everyone who has AD must be cared for by someone else. Patients and their caregivers travel a frightening and ever-changing road. But finding information and support helps ease the difficult journey.

TREATING ALZHEIMER'S

To date, no treatment exists to cure or stop the spread of Alzheimer's. As much as scientists know about the condition, AD remains difficult to predict and treat. But treatments are available. Some seem to delay the start of the disease. Others alter how the disease unfolds. Keeping up with new drugs and studies is important for AD patients and their families.

Medicine

Several treatments slow or improve signs of AD, at least for a while. The U.S. government has approved four medicines for use by Alzheimer's patients. All four come from a class of drugs known as **cholinesterase inhibitors**. None of these stops the disease from advancing. But they increase the amount of acetylcholine in the brain, since the brains of many AD patients have low levels of the protein. This protein increases

Regular appointments with a doctor can help Alzheimer's patients. The doctor can monitor the progression of the disease and offer support and advice.

the flow of messages among brain cells. Having normal levels of acetylcholine helps some patients remember, understand, talk, and behave better.

Not all patients benefit from cholinesterase inhibitors. Many experience common side effects such as **nausea** and tiredness. Improvements from the cholinesterase inhibitors usually only lasts a few months. But, many patients prefer having even small amounts of extra quality time.

Other medicines treat changes in emotions and behavior. Around 20 to 40 percent of people with AD show signs of being depressed. Different medications target **depression** and the anxiety, sleep problems, and imaginary fears that come with AD. But every drug has the risk of some serious side effects. People who are taking medication for other health problems might not be able to take these drugs. Mixing powerful medication can often cause more health problems.

Some people turn to natural substances found in the body or in nature to treat the symptoms of AD. But a person should always talk to his or her doctor before taking any sort of medication. A National Institute on Aging study showed that Vitamin E and a drug called selegeline slowed the worsening of daily living skills in AD patients. Both drugs worked equally well, but Vitamin E resulted in fewer side effects. Many doctors recommend Vitamin E to their AD patients. They believe it boosts the brain's natural ability to stop attacks from damaging substances. Many doctors also suggest folate and vitamin B12 to lessen memory loss.

Ginkgo biloba is a type of tree. For centuries, other nations have used parts of the tree to treat memory problems, swelling, and poor blood flow. Studies in the United States have shown that the extract improves thinking, memory, and behavior in people who have AD.

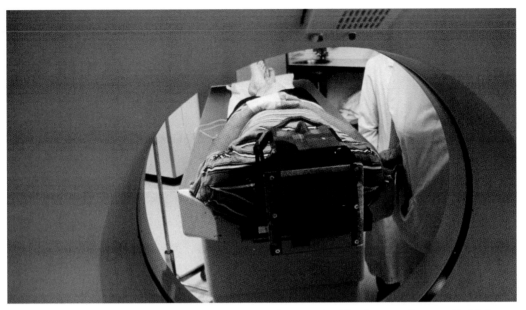

Part of treating Alzheimer's Disease is going to for regular checkups and tests. Multiple PET scans are often done at different times to track brain functions.

But more research is needed to discover what role ginkgo plays in preventing or delaying AD. Similar research is ongoing for the moss extract huperzine A and a fat from cow brains called phosphatidylserine. Both might help to treat Alzheimer's symptoms, but both require more study before they will be approved for patients.

New Ideas about Medicine

Scientists are hopeful that everyday drugs like aspirin can prevent AD. Aspirin is one of many anti-inflammatory drugs that reduce swelling. Scientists believe that brain plaques and tangles cause swelling. Now they want to know if anti-inflammatory drugs can prevent brain swelling from AD.

Two studies, one from Holland and one in the United States, find that taking an anti-inflammatory regularly for two years greatly reduces chances of developing AD. Based on this information, studies are underway to see if anti-inflammatory drugs help patients who already have AD. Early results are mixed. As with most areas of AD, more study is needed.

The United States government currently funds a seven-year project to test the ability of anti-inflammatory drugs to prevent plaques from forming. Efforts are also underway to study whether B vitamins and other drugs can help block proteins and chemicals that produce plaques and tangles.

Renewed Brain Cells. Up until 1999, scientists believed that once brain cells die, they are gone forever. As the brain loses its abilities to

Aspirin helps ease headaches and sore muscles, but scientists think that it might also treat the symptoms of AD.

function—such as in AD—the body stops working. With time, the person will die. New studies explore the brain's ability to move nerve cells from one part of the brain into another. Research on monkeys and rats shows that new cells can form in certain parts of the brain. These new cells can migrate or move to another cell.

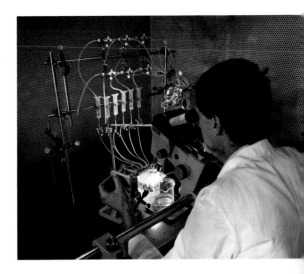

Someday scientists might be able to successfully manipulate (change) brain cells so that they can replace the cells damaged by AD.

For now, many questions need to be answered about new cell growth. Can new cells replace those that die? Will the new cells take over the jobs of the dead cells? Or do the new cells take on new and different jobs? If scientists discover that the brain uses new cells, perhaps one day they can discover how to replace those lost during AD.

Making Lifestyle Changes

A healthy lifestyle has been shown to slow signs of aging and Alzheimer's Disease. Proof of the importance of healthful living comes from two ground-breaking studies. One study tracks activities of Catholic priests and nuns from about thirty religious communities in a dozen states. After four and a half years, the more mentally active people have experienced 47 percent fewer signs of AD.

Similar results occur from another study of 678 Catholic nuns ages 75 to 106. The nuns have kept diaries since 1991. They write about everything that concerns their physical and mental health. In addition, people from both studies donate their brains after death for research.

So far, the nun study is the longest, most careful study of aging and AD. Comparing the nuns' diaries with studies of their brains confirms that higher education increases life span more than three years. It also contributes to slower aging. The study showed that positive thinking produces similar results. Controlling one's weight reduces the AD risks and better language skills decrease the chance of developing AD.

Participants from these groups provide clues to AD that researchers could not find elsewhere. This is because the nuns usually live together so they share similar lifestyles, activities, and foods. Because they tend to stay in one community forever, they are easy to follow and test. Their willingness to take part in these studies provides a lot of information about factors that affect AD.

HELPING THE PERSON WITH ALZHEIMER'S

Most people with AD try to handle legal and money matters before they lose the ability to make decisions. Laws vary from state to state, and everyone has different money arrangements. Lawyers help those with early AD identify their rights under law. They advise people how to arrange bill paying and bank accounts. They prepare papers that transfer decision-making rights to someone else. This allows a caregiver to make health-care decisions and manage household business when the person with AD becomes too disabled to act.

Safety

Home can be a dangerous place for people with AD. They need plain surroundings without harmful objects, such as guns, knives, and matches. Trying to keep things the same when reorganizing living space is important for people with AD. Favorite items should be kept in sight for comfort. Clutter, such as loose cords, rugs, and figurines, should be hidden to reduce the risk of injury. Expensive items are placed some-where safe, so they cannot be lost or accidentally destroyed.

Maintaining a steady routine is important to relieve anxiety from AD. Regular bedtimes can ease sleep problems. Some AD patients feel better or are more active during certain times of

Even as motor (movement) skills begin to worsen, Alzheimer's patients should try to continue to be active.

the day. To make the day easier, difficult tasks should be scheduled during the person's best time of the day. As AD worsens, caregivers—the people taking care of the AD patient—may take knobs off outside doors and put a lock on the bedroom door to prevent wandering. They may add special devices to keep the oven and stove off.

Taking Care of Mental Health

Sadly, AD brings a series of losses. People with AD eventually stop driving. They stop working. They lose interest in hobbies they once enjoyed. They forget people who they had known for a long time.

Those who eat a healthy diet and keep mentally active stand a better chance against dementia that interferes with the everyday joys of life. Several studies found that participating in activities that demand alertness offers some protection against memory loss.

Keeping mentally active is important even in late-stage AD. But familiar activities need adjusting as skills become more uneven. Someone who cannot talk may still be able to play a favorite sport or game. Someone who cannot wash clothes can still help to fold them and put them away. Like most people, those with AD enjoy challenges.

When speech becomes affected by the disease, some patients may see a speech therapist. Pictures cards and games are often used to encourage patients to remember and say different words. Being able to communicate with others can ease some of the frustration an AD patient feels.

Activities that Reduce the Risk of Developing Dementia

....

Nothing can stop AD. But mental activity can slow memory loss that the disease causes. Here are some mentally demanding leisure activities.

- Crossword puzzles
- Reading
- Card games
- Chess
- Board games
- Playing an instrument
- Watching films
- Engaging in discussions

HELPING CARETAKERS

At some point, people with AD need others to help them carry out their daily activities. Those who have families usually live at home for much of their disease. Partners and children of patients account for 70 percent of caregivers.

The strain of caring for someone with AD can be crushing. Patients cannot communicate. They behave oddly. They need constant watching to stay safe. As AD robs them of more skills, their care becomes a full-time job. Caregivers often give up paying jobs, social life, and free time to nurse a family member who may act like a stranger.

Gathering Information

No one can be fully prepared for the loss that accompanies AD. Roles within the family change as the caregiver takes charge. Life turns upside down with each new behavioral change AD brings. Reactions to specific behaviors vary with family members. Because every situation is different, no one plan works for every family.

Many caregivers find that getting up-to-date information helps them navigate the difficult AD journey. Knowing the range of problems and how they progress lessens the sting of surprise. Gathering the latest information allows patients and caregivers to make better health choices, find assistance, and plan ahead to meet each new stage.

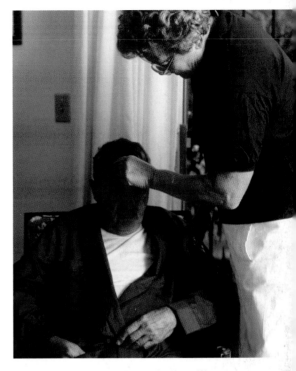

At some point, all AD patients will need help doing simple tasks such as combing their hair or brushing their teeth.

The Alzheimer's Association, a national volunteer organization, operates a Safe Return Program. Safe Return is for people with AD who wander and get lost. This nationwide program helps find lost AD patients. It alerts caregivers and local police so that the patients can be brought home safely. Since 1993, the program has registered over 100,000 people with AD. Patients wear bracelets, necklaces, or clothing labels with

The High Cost of AD

....

Alzheimer's Disease takes a toll on every-one. The illness robs patients of the ability to live life fully. AD also puts great stress on others who deal with the condition. But the monetary costs are also very high. The disease can last from two to twenty years. Families spend an average of $12,500 a year to care for a loved one at home. Living arrangements outside the home can range between $40,000 to $75,000 a year.

The cost of AD affects the entire nation. Alzheimer's Disease causes national losses of $80 billion to $100 billion a year. More than half the cost comes from lost wages (the amount paid for a job) of family members who leave work to care for someone with AD. The rest goes to the high price of medicines and long-term care outside the home.

The good news is that such high num-bers force the U.S. government to deal with these issues. Government and private groups spend $700,000 a year for research to study the disease. The National Institute on Aging funds several studies that search for causes and treatments of AD.

the Safe Return toll-free phone number and identifying infor-mation about who they are. Safe Return has recovered almost 8,000 wanderers.

Support Groups

Each family member reacts differently to AD. Those who shoulder most of the burden can become physically and mentally exhausted. They may go through stages of sadness and anger. Many find it difficult to cope with a disease that steals a partner or parent and destroys everyone's lives.

Younger children and grand-children harbor their own range of emotions about AD. Younger people may feel sadness about the disease. They may not understand what is happening.

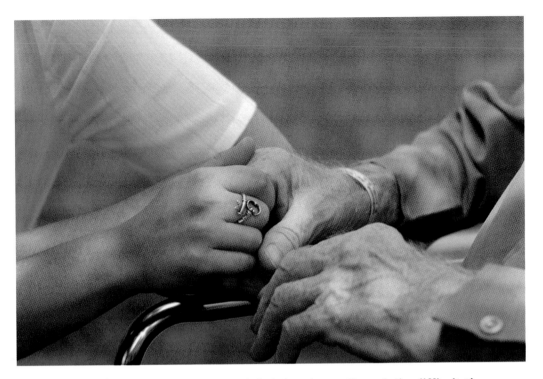

Emotional support helps AD patients and their loved ones through the difficult times.

If the patient lives with them, children may become jealous of the attention the illness requires. They may feel angry or embarrassed at someone who acts so strangely. Afterward, they feel guilty for their anger. Some refuse to share thoughts and feelings with their parents. They do not want to add to their parents burden and sadness. But sharing and expressing emotions is important. Many young people—and older people as well—do not know how to react to or deal with the illness of a loved one.

All family members can benefit from support groups. The meetings provide safe places to talk about feelings, share ideas, and find support. But demands of someone with AD may prevent normal conversations. Support may need to come from trained therapists.

The local branches of the Alzheimer's Associations offer support groups for adults and children. Hospitals and other health centers may also offer counseling and support groups. Group members can connect with other families going through similar experiences.

Additional Help

Many families hire outside help to come into their home. These nurses or health aides can help the AD patient with daily activities. This gives family members a chance to take a break. It can also help families feel a little less frustrated with the demands of managing the disease. Local branches of the Alzheimer's Association, hospitals, and medical centers keep lists of funding sources and aides to hire.

Adult day care programs provide another way to give patients and their caregivers time apart. With adult day care, the patient leaves home for a program at another location. Several people with AD take part in guided activities designed for their needs. Days are divided into simple routines of exercise, music, crafts, and other fun projects. Activities are planned based on the individual's abilities. Day care programs keep a patient's mind and body active.

Some families look to living arrangements outside the home for their relative with AD. A few hospitals and nursing homes offer the choice of short-term overnight stays. At some point, the idea of long-term care may arise. Nursing homes provide round-the-clock assistance from staff trained to deal with AD. They offer routine activities in settings that are safe for large numbers of people who have AD.

People today know much more about how Alzheimer's works than at any time since its discovery almost 100 years ago. One day they will understand what triggers AD and they can plan better ways to recognize the problem earlier and slow or eliminate the disease. Until then, however, the dedicated caregivers, families, and Alzheimer's sufferers will continue with their lives, working hard to maintain dignity, support, and love during the course of this very difficult disease.

GLOSSARY

abnormal—Not normal.

acetylcholine—A neurotransmitter that is important for memory.

anxiety—Feelings of fear or worry.

cholinesterase inhibitors—A group of drugs that boosts the brain's supply of acetylcholine.

dementia—A condition that involves the worsening of memory, thinking skills, and behaviors.

depression—A medical disorder with symptoms that include sadness, tiredness, and hopelessness.

diagnose—To identify an illness based on results of physical and mental tests.

folate—A vitamin that is good for cell growth. Low levels of folate in the blood may contribute to memory loss and confusion.

genes—Tiny parts of cells. Genes determine traits and characteristics of a plant or animal. Genes are passed on from parent to child.

ginkgo biloba—A type of tree. Its parts are used to treat memory problems, swelling, and poor blood flow.

nausea—A sick feeling in the stomach.

neurotransmitters—Chemicals that carry messages across gaps between nerve cells.

nutrients—Substances needed by living things for life and growth.

plaques—In the brain, clumps of material that interfere with brain functions.

proteins—Substances found in living cells of plants and animals. Proteins are needed for cells to do their jobs.

spinal tap—A medical test performed on fluid from the spine.

spine—The column of bones running down a person's back. The spine protects the spinal cord (a thick cord of nerve tissue), which is surrounded by fluid.

symptom—A sign that indicates the presence of a disease or illness.

tangles—Twisted threadlike substances in the brain. They prevent messages from traveling between nerve cells.

vaccine—A substance that is used to prevent illness or disease.

virus—A tiny particle that causes illness or disease.

FIND OUT MORE

Organizations

Alzheimer's Association

225 North Michigan Ave.
Suite 1700
Chicago, IL 60601
1-800-272-3900
http://www.alz.org

Alzheimer's Disease Education and Referral (ADEAR) Center

P.O. Box 8250
Silver Springs, MD 20907
1-800-438-4380
http://www.alzheimers.org

National Institute on Aging

Building 31, Room 5C27
31 Center Drive, MSC 2292
Bethesda, MD 20892
http://www.nia.nih.gov

Books

Gold, Susan Dudley. *Alzheimer's Disease*. Berkeley Heights, NJ: Enslow Publishers, 2000.

Hinnefled, Joyce. *Everything You Need to Know When Someone You Love Has Alzheimer's Disease*. New York: Rosen Publishing Group, 1994.

Park, Barbara. *The Graduation of Jake Moon*. New York: Atheneum Books for Young Readers, 2000.

Shawver, Margaret. *What's Wrong with Grandma? A Family's Experience with Alzheimer's*. Amherst, NY: Prometheus Books, 1996.

Turkington, Carol. *The Encyclopedia of Alzheimer's Disease*. New York: Facts on File, 2003.

Webber, Barbara. *Alzheimer's Disease*. San Diego, CA: Kidhaven Press, 2004.

Web Sites

About Alzheimer's
(American Health Assistance Foundation)
http://www.ahaf.org/alzdis/about/adabout.htm

Alzheimer's Disease—Neuroscience for Kids
http://faculty.washington.edu/chudler/alz.html

Helping Children Understand Alzheimer's Disease
(Alzheimer Society of Canada)
http://www.alzheimer.ca/english/care/children.htm

Children of Aging Parents
http://www.caps4caregivers.org

Eldercare Locator
http://www.eldercare.gov

The Forgetting—A Portrait of Alzheimer's
http://www.pbs.org/theforgetting

INDEX

Page numbers for illustrations are in **boldface**

ABOUT THE AUTHOR

Marlene Targ Brill writes about many topics, from history and biographies to sports, world peace, and tooth fairies. Her favorite topics involve ways to help people become healthier. When she was growing up, Marlene loved learning about the body. She came from a family of pharmacists who prepared and sold medicine to make people feel better. At one time, she wanted to be a nurse. But she became a teacher of children who had special needs instead. Now she writes about special needs and other health care topics, such as AD, for children and adults. She lives near Chicago with her husband, Richard, and daughter, Alison.